P9-BUI-876

MONROE HIGH
LIBRARY

THE ETRUSCANS
An Unsolved Mystery

Other books by Elizabeth Honness

The Great Gold Piece Mystery
Mystery of the Diamond Necklace
Mystery at the Doll Hospital
Mystery of the Auction Trunk
Mystery in the Square Tower
Mystery of the Wooden Indian
Mystery of the Secret Message
Mystery of the Hidden Face
Mystery of the Pirate's Ghost
Mystery at the Villa Caprice
Mystery of the Maya Jade

THE
ETRUSCANS

An Unsolved
Mystery

by Elizabeth Honness

J. B. Lippincott Company
Philadelphia and New York

Thanks are also due the Art Reference Bureau of Ancram, N.Y., for permission to reproduce the photographs by Alinari of Rome and Florence on the cover of this book and on pages 18, 19, 39, 48, 49, 53, 54, 57, 58, 61, 64, 69, 74, 93, 98, 99, 101, 103, 113, 119; the Metropolitan Museum of Art for the photographs on pages 26 (Fletcher Fund, 1938), 59 top (purchased by subscription, 1895), 59 bottom (Harris Brisbane Dick Fund, 1940); the University of Pennsylvania Museum for the photographs on pages 73, 82 and for permission to reproduce the silhouettes of Greek vases on page 72; the Lerici Foundation of Milan and Rome for the photographs on pages 17, 110 from M. Moretti, *La Tomba Martini-Marescotti* (Milano: Lerici Editori, 1966), and for the photographs on pages 94, 95, 105, 107, 108, 109; and to St. Martin's Press, Inc., Edward Arnold, Ltd., the Macmillan Company of Canada, Ltd., and Rowohlt Verlag Gmb H, Hamburg, for permission to reproduce from Otto-Wilhelm von Vacano's *The Etruscans in the Ancient World* the line drawings on pages 22, 25, 34, 47, 63, 70.

Maps on pages 24, 85 by Lili Cassel Wronker.

U.S. Library of Congress Cataloging in Publication Data

Honness, Elizabeth Hoffman, birth date
  The Etruscans; an unsolved mystery.

  SUMMARY: Describes the civilization that flourished on the Italian peninsula some 500 years before Christ.
  Bibliography: p.
  1. Civilization, Etruscan—Juvenile literature. [1. Civilization, Etruscan] I. Title.
DG223.H65   913.37'5'02   72-1272
ISBN-0-397-31266-0

Copyright © 1972 by Elizabeth Honness McKaughan

All rights reserved

Printed in the United States of America

First edition

For Margaret and John Keats
who helped me pursue the Etruscans
in the hill towns of Italy

ACKNOWLEDGMENTS

Sincere and appreciative thanks are due to Dr. Kenneth Matthews, Lecturer in Classical Archaeology at the University of Pennsylvania and Director of Education at the University Museum, for his critical reading of my manuscript; to Eunice Blake Bohanon, friend and former editor, for her valuable and helpful suggestions; to Carlo M. Lerici for his graciousness in receiving me in Rome and his generosity in giving me many photographs; and to Dr. Lucia Cavagnaro Vanoni of the Lerici Foundation for her kindly assistance.

Contents

THE ETRUSCANS
An Unsolved Mystery

Who were the Etruscans?

Who were these long-lost people who built cities for their dead which still can be explored, but whose shining cities for the living have vanished from the earth?

This is a question archaeology attempts to answer, but the mystery of Etruscan origins and language is still unresolved.

I

Buried Treasure

An Italian peasant tilling a field near Vulci in the Tuscany region of Italy in 1828 felt the handles of his plow quiver and jerk as the blade caught on something hard. The mild-eyed oxen drawing the plow turned their great heads in puzzlement. At a word from their master they pulled mightily but the plowshare refused to budge.

The peasant let go the handles of the plow and went to investigate. He found that the plow's sharp blade had pierced through the rock ceiling of a huge subterranean cavern. The air that wafted up from it was fetid and chill with the unmistakable odor of decay.

For a moment he was struck with awe and fear. He had heard of the Etruscans, a vanished people who first lived there eight hundred years before Christ. He knew that their custom was to bury their dead in underground chambers and to surround them with treasure for their use in the afterworld. Undoubtedly he had chanced upon a concealed tomb.

Only a year before, two tombs had been discovered in Tarquinia, a short distance to the south. Carved out of the volcanic rock called *tufa* which undergirds that land, these had yielded riches in the form of gold jewelry, decorated vases, bronze figures, and—most notable of all— vivid wall paintings with strange-looking inscriptions in a language that could not be deciphered.

Much of the land around Vulci was owned at that time by Lucien Bonaparte, the prince of Cannino, a brother of Napoleon. The peasant's find started a rash of exploration, hasty and unscientific, a grand treasure hunt that netted the prince more than two thousand priceless Greek vases for his private collection. Other rich landowners of the region also profited. They took only the most rare and valuable objects, discarding or destroying the rest. The tombs were then filled up or closed over. No drawings were made of their interiors, no inventory taken of their contents. Incalculable damage had been done. Worst of all, from the point of view of archaeology, was the failure to keep records or to document the evidence.

Frescoed tombs with lovely wall paintings had been discovered in the previous century, and other Etruscan tombs had been opened by accident during work in the fields as early as the fourteenth and fifteenth centuries. Artists, including the master Michelangelo, had gone to them for inspiration.

A Greek amphora for wine, discovered in a tomb in the necropolis of Cerveteri, showing grape-picking satyrs watched over by Dionysius.

Superb bronze sculptures were unearthed in those early times, among them the famous she-wolf known as the Capitoline Wolf because she is in the Capitoline Museum in Rome. Where she was discovered is not known. It is known, however, that the figures of the babies, Romulus and Remus—who, according to the myth, are credited with founding Rome—were added to the original Etruscan work during the Renaissance, which began in Italy in the fourteenth century and lasted three hundred years.

17

Romulus and Remus, shown being nursed by the she-wolf, were twin grandsons of the rightful king of a tribe in the Alban hills whose throne had been usurped by his brother. According to the legend, this wicked man, fearing the boys' future claim on the throne, ordered them drowned. They were placed in a basket near the overflowing River Tiber which carried them downstream. As the flood waters receded, the basket came to rest on land, and the babies' cries were heard by a thirsty she-wolf who had come to the river to drink. She let them suck her milk and mothered them until they were found by a herdsman who took them to his hut and protected them. Years later, when their own grandfather regained power and acknowledged them as his heirs, they decided to found a settlement at the spot near the river where they were found. But they quarreled about who should govern their new town and Remus was killed by Romulus. The city became Rome.

An equally famous statue, the Chimera, was found in Arezzo, some miles south of Florence, in 1553. It is a fierce-looking mythological creature with a lion's head. An antelope with a hooked beak grows from its back, and it has a serpent tail. A bronze Minerva, goddess of wisdom and the arts, came to light the following year. Both are among the glories of the Archaeological Museum in Florence.

During the eighteenth century two scholars, a French and a German, made efforts to assess what was then known about the Etruscans. Imaginative accounts were also written, but it was not until after the farmer's find in

Bronze chimera, discovered in Arezzo in 1553.

1828 that the rediscovery of Etruria began, stimulated by the uncovering of countless works of art. Many of these are in museums in America and in several countries of Europe as well as in Italy.

In the nineteenth century the second phase of the reclamation of Etruscan cities of the dead began. Institutions and private individuals provided money for the work of exploring the great Etruscan cemeteries and necropolises, particularly around the coastal areas where Cerveteri, Tarquinia, and Vulci are located.

Early in the twentieth century the Italian government took a hand, creating a Department of Architecture and Fine Arts and sponsoring the intensive explorations which have enriched Italy's national and local museums. Archaeology has been aided by the invention of new tools and methods which save time and labor.

For more than 150 years now the search has gone on, with the thirst for knowledge supplanting the greed of individuals. Only a small fraction of the burial sites have been touched by modern excavators. There are acres of tombs, some of them in the form of tumuli, or mounds, still concealing knowledge needed to reconstruct the civilization of ancient Etruria, and awaiting the picks and shovels of the archaeologists.

II

The Mystery:
Who Were the Etruscans?
Where Did They Come From?

The peninsula of Italy thrusts downward from the underside of Europe like an elongated high-heeled boot wading into the Mediterranean with the island of Sicily broken off from the tip of its toe. The Alps and the Dolomites form a gigantic mountain barrier to the north. On the east its shores are washed by the Adriatic Sea, on the west by the Ligurian and the Tyrrhenian seas, with the Gulf of Taranto lapping at its instep.

Eons ago, when the world was being formed, the Apennines were heaved up in a great volcanic convulsion. They form a spiny ridge across the top of the boot and extend down its length. Beech, oak, larch, chestnut, pine, and juniper clothe its heights. Its lower slopes are wreathed with the silvery green of olive trees and punctuated with the dark spires of cypress.

To the north the River Po, fed by mountain snows,

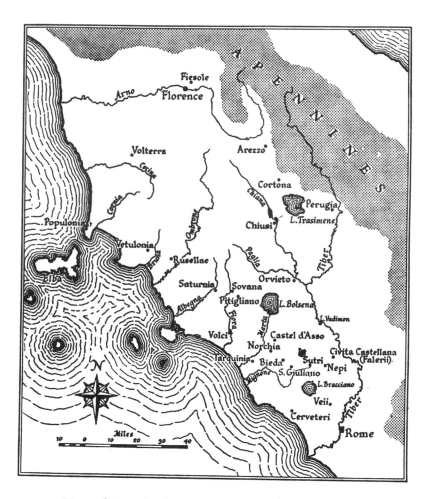

Map of Etruria showing the chief Etruscan towns.

flows south and east to the Adriatic. Other great rivers, notably the Arno and the Tiber, have their source in the high mountain backbone of the land. There are deep glacial lakes in the north, and numerous lakes in the craters of extinct volcanoes farther south. Near the beautiful Bay

22

of Naples, Vesuvius rears its blue bulk against the sky and reminds one of its menace by sending puffs of smoke into the air.

Geography thus had a great deal to do with isolating Italy from the ferment of civilization that had taken place in other Mediterranean lands. Even as far back as 3000 B.C., during the Copper and Bronze Ages, Egypt, Mesopotamia, Asia Minor, and Crete, an island in the Aegean Sea, had brilliant cultures, while the Italian peninsula still slept in the darkness of prehistory.

It was not until the Iron Age dawned in Italy, about 1000 B.C., that the awakening began. Meanwhile, northern peoples had invaded Italy through Alpine passes, and peoples from the Balkans had come across the Adriatic. They intermingled with the native tribes, imposing on them many of their own primitive customs. But none of these early inhabitants, these pre-Etruscans, left written records on which history can be based. It is only through archaeology that knowledge of them has come to light.

Lacking written records, archaeology must reconstruct the past from the durable objects—the leftovers of older civilizations, uncovered by the spade. The archaeologists painstakingly fit together the bits and pieces they have retrieved and from them try to paint a picture of the life long ago. It is scientific detective work of a high order.

Excavations by archaeologists brought knowledge of the first people in Italy to be associated with the Iron Age. They were called Villanovans, from the town of that name near Bologna in the north. They knew how to

MAP SHOWING ETRUSCAN EXPANSION AND TERRITORIES OF OTHER TRIBES

ETRUSCAN EXPANSION

CARTHAGINIAN COLONIZATION

GREEK COLONIZATION

LIGURIANS

LIGURIAN SEA

ETRUSCANS

CORSICA

ELBA

PO R.

Mantua
Adria
Spina
Felsina
Marzabotto
Ravenna
Florence
Rimini
Volterra
ARNO
Arretium
Cortona
Populonia
Perugia
Vetulonia
Rusellae
Clusium
Volsini
Alalia
Vulci
Tarquinii
Veii
Caere
Rome
Praeneste
LATINS
UMBRIANS
SAMNITES
SABINES

ADRIATIC SEA

TYRRHENIAN SEA

SARDINIA

Cumae
Paestum
CAMPAGNA
Tarentum

Sybaris

Crotona

SICILIAN STRAITS
Locri
Rhegium

Syracuse

SICILY

use and work iron. They cremated their dead, placing the ashes in urn-shaped receptacles which they covered with small inverted cuplike lids. Later on these lids were replaced by helmets with high crests of laminated bronze, apparently intended in a crude way to represent the heads of the deceased. This was the beginning of funerary sculpture which later the Etruscans were to perfect.

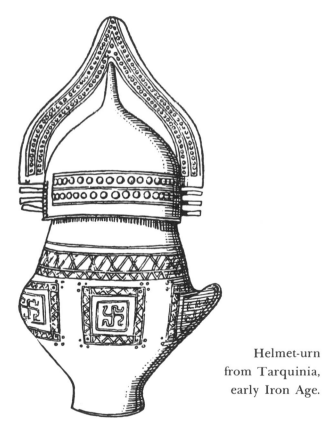

Helmet-urn
from Tarquinia,
early Iron Age.

Other early people of the same period placed the ashes of their dead in hut urns—little hut-shaped houses made of ceramics or bronze, modeled after the huts they had occupied when alive. These were deposited in pits dug out of the rock or the ground and beside them were placed offerings. For men there were weapons, helmets, iron daggers and swords; for the women, the bronze clasps or safety pins called *fibulae,* which held together the material of their garments. In addition there were jewels of amber and bronze, combs, needles, spindles for winding yarn—everything that would be needed for their comfort and for daily tasks in the afterworld.

Cinerary hut urn in bronze, seventh century B.C.

Burial customs and offerings left for the dead thus reveal much about the people who lived in past ages. The archaeologist has to be a grave-robber in order to find out about ancient people, but he is probably the only grave-robber who is not condemned for his activity, because the nameless people whose graves he violates have long become forgotten dust.

The Etruscan civilization which followed and grew upon the Villanovans was the first to flower in Italy after the Iron Age. It was well established by 700 B.C. and reached its peak five hundred years before Christ. We know from ancient Greek and Roman writers that its people were called Tyrrhenians, or Tyrsenians, and Lydians, and that they referred to themselves as *Rasena*.

Did they come from Lydia in Asia Minor where the wealthy King Croesus once ruled? His name has long been part of our language; we say, "As rich as Croesus." That he was vastly rich was confirmed in 1968 by the discovery of gold refineries in the lost city of Sardia, capital of Lydia, where Croesus was king twenty-five centuries ago.

Or did the Etruscans develop from a mingling of ethnic backgrounds of Stone Age people native to Italy itself?

The Greek historian Herodotus, who lived and wrote during the fifth century B.C., was one of several ancient writers who believed the Etruscans came from Lydia. His theory is still considered valid by some scholars.

We do know that the Lydians were the first people to

use gold and silver coinage. Herodotus tells us in his *Histories:*

> They also claim to have invented the games which are now commonly played both by themselves and the Greeks. These games are supposed to have been invented at the time when they sent a colony to settle in Tyrrhenia, and the story is that in the reign of Atys [who preceded Croesus by several centuries] . . . the whole of Lydia suffered a severe famine. For a time the people lingered on as patiently as they could but later, when there was no improvement, they began to look for something to alleviate their misery. Various expedients were devised: for instance, the invention of dice, knucklebones and ball games . . . to help them endure their hunger . . . one day playing so continuously that they had no time to think of food, and eating on the next without playing at all. They managed to live like this for eighteen years. There was no remission of their suffering—indeed it grew worse so the King divided the population into two groups and determined by drawing lots which should emigrate and which should remain at home. He appointed himself to rule the section whose lots determined that they should remain, and his son Tyrrhenus to command the emigrants. The lots were drawn, and one section went down to the coast at Smyrna, where they built vessels, put aboard all their household effects and sailed in search of a livelihood elsewhere. They passed many countries and finally reached Umbria in the north of Italy where they settled and still live to

this day. Here they changed their name from Lydians to Tyrrhenians, after the King's son, Tyr-
rhenus, who was their leader.

The Tyrrhenian Sea that sweeps the western shore of
Italy also takes its name from him.

The people of ancient times accepted Herodotus's account, and classical writers frequently referred to the
Etruscans as Lydians, but some scholars think Herodotus
was retelling a legend rather than relating a historical
fact.

His version was first questioned four centuries later in
the time of the Roman emperor Augustus by a man
named Dionysius who came from Halicarnassus, the
Greek town in southwest Asia Minor where Herodotus
was born nearly a half century earlier. Dionysius's work
on Roman antiquities maintains that the Etruscans were
native or indigenous to Italy. He based this opinion on a
document by a fifth-century B.C. Lydian author named
Xanthus who, writing of the Lydians of that earlier period, made no mention of an emigration by them. Dionysius also points out that they did not speak the same language as the Lydians, did not have the same laws, did not
worship the same gods, and did not resemble any other
ancient people either in language or customs.

These two opposing theories have been argued down
to the present day. Raymond Bloch, a noted French archaeologist and specialist in the science of inscriptions
and epitaphs, is considered an authority on the Etrus-

cans. He believes that the theory of an Oriental or Eastern origin has validity. He points out that there are many similarities between Etruscan customs and ways of life and those of the people of ancient Asia Minor. Even their own national name *Rasena* is found in closely similar forms in dialects of Asia Minor, as is the Greek name for the Etruscans, *Tyrrhenoi*. Many Etruscan customs, religious beliefs, and artistic skills can be connected with the Orient.

One mark of Etruscan civilization that had a parallel in Lydian social structure was the position of equality their women shared with men. The Etruscan women are frequently shown in tomb frescoes reclining beside their husbands at the banqueting tables; they attended athletic contests and chariot races. In contrast, the Greek women were kept in the background subordinate to their husbands.

Archaeologists today believe that there may be truth in both opposing theories of origin. Possibly successive small groups of emigrants from Asia Minor came to the sunny shores of the Tyrrhenian Sea, subdued the native populations—the farmers, workmen, soldiers and artisans—and took for themselves the positions of power. And possibly from that time on, an amalgam or mingling of native and foreign strains produced the Etruscans. But no one knows for certain.

III

A Conspiracy of History

At the period of their greatest power, between 600 and 500 B.C., the Etruscans dominated Italy from the plains of the River Po in the north to the River Tiber and even farther south. The province of present-day Tuscany was the heart of their domain. When Rome was only a cluster of small villages on seven hills in an area called Latium, the great cities of Etruria, the land of the Etruscans, were centers of culture and art.

Sometime before 600 B.C. a man, the son of an Etruscan mother and a Greek noble who had emigrated from Corinth to Tarquinia, went to Rome at the urging of his wife Tanaquil, an Etruscan prophetess. There he became a citizen, taking the name of Lucius Tarquinius Priscus, which means Tarquin the Elder, and rose to a high position. In 616 B.C., on the death of the king, he either seized power or was elected king of Rome. During the reign of this first Etruscan king, the warlike Samnite tribes were defeated and all of Latium was brought under the control of Rome. Two other Etruscan kings followed him. Altogether the rule of these kings lasted one hundred years, during which time the villages on seven hills became one large city, and the influence of the Etruscans was great.

Sons of wealthy Roman families were sent to Caere, present-day Cerveteri, to be educated and to absorb some of the superior culture of the Etruscans. The Roman historian Livy tells us that up to the end of the fourth century B.C. young Romans studied Etruscan literature just as they did Greek.

The first walls around Rome for defense were built by the Etruscans. The third Etruscan king, Tarquinius Superbus, brought builders and engineers from all over Etruria to help erect the temple to Jupiter on the Capitoline Hill, the highest of the seven hills, which was the religious center of the city. They worked, too, on the gigantic Circus Maximus where horses and boxers, many from Etruria, provided entertainment and where games modeled after the famous Greek games were held.

They also built the Cloaca Maxima (or great sewer) to carry off sewage from the entire city through an underground channel and empty it into the Tiber. This suggests that the Etruscans were no wiser about pollution in their day than people of the present time. The marshy ground below the Palatine Hill was also drained by the

Cloaca Maxima and became the site of the Roman Forum which was the very center of ancient Rome.

There are numerous evidences of Etruscan influence on Roman customs. The bundle of rods with an axe projecting from the center called *Fasces,* which was carried before Roman magistrates as an emblem of secular authority, came from the Etruscans. The laurel wreath, the chair of state, the toga, and the use of purple to indicate power can be traced to them. Even the gladiatorial games are a changed version of the funeral games with which the Etruscans honored their dead.

These people excelled in the crafts of pottery and jewelry, casting in bronze, and the arts of sculpture and painting, but they left no body of literature. That an Etruscan literature once existed we know from references by classical writers. Fragments of writing from Etruscan sacred books have been preserved. These were translated into Latin by Tarquinius Priscus. Only a few brief passages of this translation have survived in the writings of Latin classical authors such as Seneca and Pliny the Elder. They dealt with the extraordinary signs and natural wonders that revealed the wishes of the gods. These sacred books and the priests who interpreted them exerted a tremendous influence on Roman paganism.

Ten thousand or more inscriptions have been found engraved or painted on mirrors, chests, vases, sculptures, paintings, tiles, columns, funerary urns, and sarcophagi. Most are limited to a few words each, and nine-tenths of them are epitaphs telling only the name of the deceased,

OAKRIDGE HIGH SCHOOL
LIBRARY

Original alphabet	Archaic inscriptions VII–V cent. B.C.	Later inscriptions IV–I cent. B.C.	Sound-Values
A	A	A	*a*
B			*(b)*
ꓶ	)	)	*c* (=*k*)
D			*(d)*
⧣	⧣	⧣	*e*
ꓱ	ꓱ	ꓶ	*v*
I	I	I	*z*
B	B	B	*h*
⊗	⊗	⊙	θ (=*th*)
I	I	I	*i*
Ж	Ж		*k*
⅃	⅃	⅃	*l*
M	M	m	*m*
ꓴ	ꓴ	n	*n*
⊞			*(s)*
O			*(o)*
ꓶ	ꓶ	ꓶ	*p*
M	M	M	*ś*
Q	Q		*q*
D	D	D	*r*
ⵑ	ⵑ	ⵑ	*s*
T	T	T	*t*
Y	Y	V	*u*
X	X.+		*ś*
Φ		Φ	φ (=*ph*)
↓		↓	χ (=*ch*)
	℥	8	*f*

The Etruscan alphabet in its original form and in its archaic and later periods, with sound values.

his parentage and age. A limited number of texts consist of more than one line, even fewer of as many as a hundred words, and only one of more than that number.

Since the Etruscans borrowed their alphabet from the Greeks of Cumae, the short inscriptions can be read with comparative ease, but these add little to our knowledge. The Etruscan language is thus still another mystery.

The longest inscription found so far is a handwritten text on twelve linen bandages wound round a mummy discovered in Alexandria, Egypt. It is now in the Zagreb Museum in Yugoslavia. The bandages were evidently a linen scroll or book put to unprecedented use. There are fifteen hundred words, but only five hundred of them differ from one another. As near as research has been able to determine, the words contain a sort of sacred calendar telling which religious ceremonies should be carried out to honor the gods. The sense of the paragraphs is known but many obscure points still baffle scholars.

A more recent discovery during excavations in the mid-1960s at Pyrgi, an ancient Etruscan port between Tarquinia and Caere, aroused great hopes. The three gold tablets or plaques found there were inscribed with texts in Etruscan and Punic, the language of the Carthaginians. But hopes were blasted when partial translations showed that the inscriptions were not identical, though each seemed to be of a dedicatory nature. If they had been parallel or identical, scholars familiar with the Punic language could have deduced the meaning of the Etruscan words in the other text.

Ancient writers compiled glossaries of Etruscan words. From them we find out that *aisar* in Etruscan meant "the gods"; *capu,* "a falcon"; *falado,* "the sky"; *lanista* (also a Roman word possibly derived from the Etruscan), "a gladiator"; *suplu,* "a flute player." Altogether the meaning of some thirty words is known. With this limited vocabulary, scholars have also some knowledge of the grammar of the language and a good understanding of its phonetics. But its relation to other Mediterranean languages is not understood.

The mystery of the Etruscan language is compounded by the lack of a body of writing to furnish a vocabulary. What is needed to aid in deciphering the language is a longer nonfunerary inscription or a parallel Etruscan-Latin text which could serve as an Etruscan Rosetta Stone providing clues to the meaning of Etruscan words.

The famous Rosetta Stone, which solved the mystery of Egyptian hieroglyphics, was found in 1799 near Rosetta, a town at one of the mouths of the Nile. Of black basalt, it bore three vertical inscriptions: one in Greek; one in a simplified form of hieroglyphs, used by Egyptian priests, called Demotic; and the third in the more complicated formal hieroglyphic picture writing. Not until this extraordinary discovery was made could Egyptian hieroglyphics be understood.

A discovery in 1885 by two young scholars of the French School in Athens produced another example of the language. It was a funeral stele or shaft of stone, found near the village of Kaminia on the island of Lemnos in the northeastern Aegean Sea almost opposite the entrance to the Dardanelles. On the stele was the profile face of a warrior with a lance, and around his head were two engraved texts. These inscriptions were in the Greek alphabet, though the language was not Greek but was later identified as close to Etruscan.

Some scholars date the stele as far back as 700 B.C., nearly two hundred years before the island was conquered by the Greeks. This suggests that the first inhabitants of Lemnos may have been Etruscans who came from nearby Asia Minor. That the early people living on the island spoke a language similar to Etruscan was further substantiated when, in the 1930s, students from the Italian School in Athens found other fragments of inscriptions written in the same language. The stele from Lemnos is now housed in a room with Etruscan vases in the Archaeological Museum in Athens.

The emperor Claudius, who ruled Rome before Nero —from A.D. 41 to 54—wrote a history of the Etruscan people in twenty volumes. His first wife was an Etruscan and helped him in this undertaking. He also compiled an Etruscan grammar. Both would be of incomparable value to scholars today, but alas, though we know these books existed, they have never been found. It is almost as though there were a conspiracy of history to blot out knowledge of this ancient people.

IV

The Land Where
They Flourished

The land where the Etruscans first flourished was bounded on the north by the Arno River. The Apennines thrust into it from the east. The Tiber and its tributary river, the Chiana, formed part of the eastern and southern boundaries. On the west, two hundred miles of coastline along the Tyrrhenian Sea provided numerous bays and inlets where ports were established. From them the Etruscans sent out their swift ships to trade with the Greek colonies in southern Italy, and with the Phoenicians in Carthage and Sardinia. They also indulged in piracy, which at that time was an accepted way of gaining wealth. The sea provided the easiest means of communication with the cities in the north. The land itself is almost like a heaving inland sea, so broken up it is with hills and mountains and deep valleys through which rush

OAKRIDGE HIGH SCHOOL LIBRARY
OAKRIDGE, OR 97463

The Land Where They Flourished

sparkling streams. Thus the inland cities were effectively separated from each other.

Wherever there was level land, wheat and other grains were grown. The Etruscans had domestic animals. Carvings in their tombs show geese and hens. Wall paintings indicate that horses, oxen, and cattle were part of their economy, as were sheep from which they spun wool for clothing. The hillsides were terraced as they are today and planted with vineyards and groves of olive trees. Numerous hot and cold mineral and sulphur springs

Interior of Tomb of the Painted Reliefs, Cerveteri. Note goose at base of column to left with kylix hanging above.

spurted from this volcanic land, and there was plenty of sweet water for drinking.

Most important to the wealth of Etruria were the mineral deposits—iron, zinc, copper, tin, and silver-bearing lead in ore-producing mountains on the mainland and on the offshore island of Elba. These were exploited by the city of Volterra and by the cities commercially associated with her, Populonia and Vetulonia. There was abundant firewood for smelting and lumber for building temples, houses, and ships.

According to Herodotus, the Etruscans first appeared in Italy as early as 1000 B.C., but the actual date is not known. Their civilization was superimposed on that of the native Villanovan and Umbrian peoples. The Etruscans built their cities on easily fortified hilltops and by 600 B.C. they had formed a loose federation of twelve city-states. Each was ruled by a priest-king called a lucumon who was chosen from among the aristocratic descendants of the first arrivals.

These first twelve city-states may be located on the map on page 22. Probably the first was Tarquinia, northwest of Rome. It is noted for the numerous tombs discovered there with painted frescoes on their walls.

Southward is Cerveteri, which was known in Etruscan times as Caere. There are three enormous necropolises, or cities of the dead, beyond the walls of the small modern town. Though inland from the sea on their high hills, both Tarquinia and Cerveteri had their own ports and prospered from a lively trade with other lands.

East of Cerveteri and just north of Rome was the wealthy city of Veii, whose later defeat by the Romans seriously weakened the Etruscan nation. Only ruins remain today.

North of Veii and in the center of the southern Etruscan territory is a large sparkling lake, Bolsena, where once Volsinii stood. It was the religious center of the federation of city-states, long vanished from man's memory until its recent discovery during excavations begun in 1964 by French archaeologists. It was here each year that delegates from the twelve cities came together at a national sanctuary, the sacred grove of the god Voltumna, to celebrate their sacred games and to confer with one another.

Further north on the Chiana River is Chiusi, called Clusium by the Romans of early times. From it the famous Lucumon Lars Porsenna of Clusium went forth to battle with the Roman Horatius at the bridge over the Tiber, an event which was celebrated in Lord Macaulay's stirring poem in the *Lays of Ancient Rome*.

East of Chiusi on the boundary of Etruscan territory are Perugia and, in a line going north, Cortona and Arezzo, called Arretium by the Etruscans. Due west of Arezzo is Volterra on its commanding outcrop of rock, where some of the original Etruscan walls still stand and indicate that the area of the ancient city was considerably larger than the Volterra of today.

South from Volterra are Vetulonia and Rusellae. Foundations of the latter have been found under the ruins of an ancient Roman town which was built over the earlier Etruscan one.

South of Rusellae and nearer the sea is Vulci, of which little remains today but a desolate windswept plateau and a noble arched bridge over the Fiora River. Built of massive blocks of native tufa stone, it demonstrates the engineering skill of the Etruscans.

Unfortunately, and to their great disadvantage, these cities never achieved political unity. Religion and language were their only ties.

Other important Etruscan towns were Populonia, on the coast southwest of Volterra; Fiesole, on a hillside above Florence; Orvieto, commanding the plain from the crest of a towering rose-red rampart of rock not unlike some of the buttes in our own West; Sovana; Saturnia; Tuscania; and Praeneste, southeast of Rome, known today as Palestrina.

Etruria was separated into three geological divisions: the southern tufa area, the northwest region of iron and metal deposits, and the Apennine valleys of the northeast. Each region had its own characteristic pattern of city and cemetery, its own style of bronze works, terra cotta, stone carving, and painting. Natural geography cut off these regions from one another and from Rome, except for the city-states of Caere and Veii, which bordered on Roman territory and later were the first to be subdued and absorbed.

The great hilltop cities that the Etruscans built, though they were marvels in their day, have vanished utterly. The Roman legions overpowered many of them, destroying and burning. Epidemics of malaria accounted for the decline and disappearance of others. That they were once Etruscan is attested by the tombs that have been found, and by other archaeological evidence.

In their places new towns grew up over the years, sometimes bearing the same names or Roman versions of the Etruscan names. Here and there a portion of a massive city wall, a bridge, or an archway remains, built of huge blocks of stone wondrously fitted together without mortar. Because of the size of the stone blocks, this form of masonry is called Cyclopean after the one-eyed giants of mythological times—the enormous Cyclops who forged thunderbolts for the god Zeus. One of them, Polyphemus, was blinded by Odysseus on his way home from the sack of Troy.

Today's traveler in Tuscany may feel that he has stumbled into a fairy tale when he comes suddenly on a hill town rising above fields of golden grain, green meadows, and terraced vineyards. Perched on a lofty height and bathed in the clear unearthly light of that region, narrow stone houses with roofs of earth-colored tile are jumbled together behind ancient walls with tawny towers soaring skyward. If the traveler had X-ray eyes which could penetrate through the various levels of civilizations below and around the town, he would soon discover that one of the earliest layers was Etruscan.

The famed Roman author Livy, who died in A.D. 17, wrote in one of his histories: "The might of the Etruscans, before the Romans rose to power, stretched widely over land and sea. . . . Such was the power of Etruria that she filled not only the land but also the sea with her fame throughout the length of Italy from the Alps to the Sicilian Straits."

V

The Cities of the Dead

Much of what we know about the Etruscans has been revealed by the cities of their dead. These were constructed underground beyond the city walls, often on a parallel hillside or plateau with a stream of water running in the ravine separating the city of the living from that of the dead.

The Etruscans practiced both inhumation and cremation. In inhumation the embalmed body was placed in a stone coffin or sarcophagus in an oblong pit carved out of stone, or on a stone couch bed within a tomb. When the body was cremated, the ashes were placed in a pottery urn. In primitive times these urns were lowered into pits hewn out of rock. At a later period, cinerary urns took the form of small sarcophagi, sometimes of translucent alabaster, with sculptured reliefs on sides and ends depicting scenes from daily life or from mythology. Figures of the deceased supporting themselves on one elbow reclined on the lids. Their bodies are foreshortened; the heads, abnormally large, are vividly realistic portraits. The men were often shown wearing thick necklaces and holding in one extended hand a shallow offering bowl called a *patera* with a raised center. Women were posed in the same attitude on the sarcophagus lids, but held mirrors or flowers.

In Chiusi and the area around that city, the early custom was to place the ashes and bits of bone from a cremated body in an urn in human form called a *canopus*. Canopic jars were earlier used in ancient Egypt to hold the entrails of embalmed bodies. The Etruscan canopic jars have head-shaped lids. The faces have huge staring eyes, gold earrings hang from the ears; the handles are in the shape of arms with hands laid on the belly of the jar. These grotesquely human-looking urns were enthroned on clay, stone, or bronze chairs which may have had some religious significance, unknown to us now.

The three great necropolises at Cerveteri are distinguished by their mound tombs (tumuli) which came into use in the seventh century B.C. Vast numbers of them extend along the funerary roads like so many giant mushrooms just pushing out of the ground. The roads, paved with stone, are worn and rutted from the wheels of the funerary carts which carried the dead to their last resting place.

The population of the town must have remained more or less constant while the cities of the dead grew and

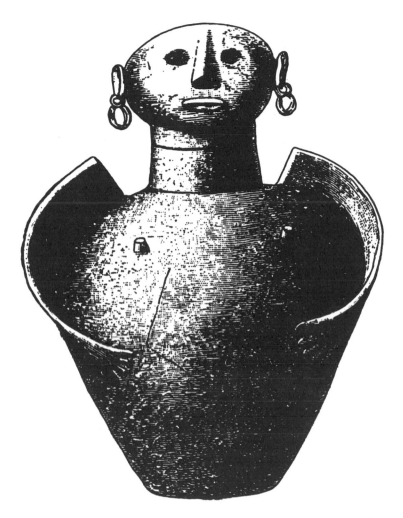

A canopus, or urn in human form, from approximately
650 B.C.

grew and spread out over more and more territory. It is
estimated that the tumuli here fill more than 140 acres in
three necropolises, though only about 6 acres of tombs
have been systematically excavated and restored.

Funereal road with Etruscan mound tombs or tumuli.

The base of each mound is girdled by a stone wall carved with moldings along the top edge. In these walls are the doorways to the tombs, reached by steps hollowed out of stone. Some tumuli have two entrances, one above the other, or can be entered from opposite sides. The burial chambers within are cut out of the tufa rock with great architectural skill in imitation of Etruscan houses. Some have peaked ceilings shaped like an upside-down V, with central beams supported by pillars. There is often an antechamber with two side rooms, but the principal tomb is at the far end, entered through another chamber with two or even three cell-like rooms beyond. These were reserved for married couples, the embalmed body of the wife frequently placed to the left of her husband. Doors and windows are decorated with stone moldings and give onto the cells which are provided with stone couches or beds hewn out of the rock.

Many of the tombs have been given names suggested by some characteristic of the interior. The Tomb of the Reliefs, for instance, is distinguished by realistic carvings

Tomb of the Alcove, Cerveteri. Note central beam with sloped ceiling and grooved pillars. Small pillars like over-turned toadstools and pedimented stone chests were usually placed outside the tomb to indicate numbers of men and women buried within.

on the pillars and walls. Some are of household utensils: cooking pots and pans, ladles, fire tongs, and hanging wine cups. Others are of animals: decorative rams' heads, geese, dogs, and a pig. Traces of the paint which originally covered them still remain. (See photo on page 39). The Tomb of the Shields and Chairs is named for the large round shields that are carved on its walls and the stone chairs with footstools that stand near the funeral beds.

Before the tumuli are small upright cylindrical stones which indicate the number of men buried inside. Stone chests with peaked tops tell the number of women.

There are also simple chamber tombs imitating the interiors of houses, with stone benches, pillars, and peaked ceilings. These are cut into the rocky sides of the ravine, or beneath the level of the necropolises on either side of the funereal roads which parallel or cross each other. In some areas, particularly near Sovana and Norchia, the rock tombs cut high on the face of the ravine walls have elaborate façades suggesting the exterior of temples.

The Etruscans seemed to believe that the dead underwent a transformation in the grave, that they became new powerful beings. Before this could happen they were helpless as babes, dependent on the care of their family before they could enter into their new life. If everything needed was provided, the spirits of the dead would be friendly guardians and protectors of the living; if not, they would become dangerous evil spirits.

"Etruscan thought was always haunted by the fate of

the dead and the other world," writes Professor Bloch in *The Etruscans*. "In Etruria the care of the dead seemed constantly to obsess the living. . . . After the burial it [the tomb] is protected by a circle of stones, or an immense flagstone sealing the entrance against the greed of man and the threat of evil spirits. There the man rested with his weapons and the women with their jewels. Thus the dead could take pleasure in their last dwelling and not return to haunt the living."

VI

"The Taste for Joyous Life" or What the Tombs Tell Us

On the dark cold walls of the underground tombs in Tarquinia, the paintings that have survived the ravages of age and dampness glow with color and vitality. Quite evidently the Etruscans enjoyed gaiety and luxury. Their women recline side by side with their husbands on banqueting couches, feasting and imbibing, while graceful and handsome slaves attend their needs. Male and female dancers entertain them, cavorting and throwing themselves wholeheartedly into the rhythms produced by the citharas (Greek lyres) and the flutes.

Highbred horses arch their necks, eager to begin the chariot races; muscular athletes and soldiers vie with each other in games and contests. Lions and leopards, dolphins and deer, wild boars and bulls—even a little mouse—have their places in the paintings along with graceful formalized trees and flowers, borders of pomegranates, and queer beasts that never existed except in primitive imaginations: winged sphinxes, hippogriffs, (fabulous winged animals, part horse and part griffin), centaurs (half horse, half man), spotted lionesses with pendant udders and long tongues hanging out.

The Greek historian Diodorus Siculus, who lived in the first century B.C. during the time of Julius Caesar, wrote, "Twice each day they [the Etruscans] spread costly tables and upon them [there is] everything that is appropriate to excessive luxury, providing gay-colored couches and having ready at hand a multitude of silver drinking cups of every description and servants-in-waiting in no small numbers; and these attendants are some of them of exceeding comeliness and others are arrayed in clothing more costly than befits the station of a slave."

Tomb of the Baron, Tarquinia. High-stepping horses and hippocampi (horses with dolphin tails) appear in pediment.

Tomb of the Lionesses, Tarquinia. Woman with castanets, dark-skinned man with wine jug in joyous dance. The hindquarters and long waving tail of one spotted lioness appear in what is shown of the pediment. Frieze of sliced-open pomegranates below.

Slaves were men and women captured in wars or bought at auction and often were high-born individuals.

Indeed, other ancient writers suggest that the Etruscan enjoyment of luxury and desire for pleasure contributed to their downfall. But, as Professor Bloch stated recently, "For us the Etruscan taste for joyous life within a splendid setting has had one happy result: a pictorial record unmatched in classic art. The Etruscan murals bring to vivid life a people who were in love with life and art and who, in the dwellings of their dead, have left inexhaustible testimony to their aspirations, their desires, and their joys."

The men in these lively paintings are half naked, their bodies painted earth red, a convention that did not apply to the women whose skin was painted in pale tones. They wear short embroidered kilts or brightly colored tunics called *chitons,* a garment they borrowed from the Greeks. In some paintings the men are shown wearing cloaks called *tebennos* woven of soft wool and then embroidered. This cloak was the forerunner of the Roman toga.

The women are pictured wearing tunics of lightweight sheer fabric pleated to the hems. The material is pinned at the shoulder with intricately designed pins or clasps called *fibulae.* Over these they wear thick cloaks or robes heavily embroidered in color.

The Etruscans loved shoes, and their shoes were renowned in the rest of ancient Italy. Those of the aristocrats were made of leather or embroidered material. They were long and tapered at the toe, curling up in front with the backs of the shoes cut high. They have an Oriental look as do the dome-shaped hats worn by both men and women, which were called *tutulus* and are definitely Eastern in origin. The plebs or common people wore low sandals with jointed wooden soles reinforced with bronze. Some examples of these have been found in recent excavations. Hats with wide brims were worn by servants and slaves.

Hair styles were as varied as they are today. The early Etruscan men wore pointed beards and long flowing hair. Later on, after 500 B.C., the young men's hair was worn short and they were clean-shaven, following the example of the young Greeks of that time.

The ladies indulged in a great variety of hair-dos, sometimes wearing hair piled high, at other times plaiting it into braids which rested on neck and shoulders. Curls were sometimes worn on either side of the face. Later still, the Greek style of a loose knot at the nape of the neck was adopted. Some of the frescoes of the fifth century indicate that Etruscan women even dyed their hair blond. They wore cosmetics which they kept in beautifully wrought and decorated bronze coffers called *cista,* similar to the ones in which they stored their jewels.

Hand mirrors of burnished bronze, engraved on their backs with scenes from Greek myths and legends, were part of the tomb furnishings for women. More than fifteen hundred decorated hand mirrors have been found in Etruscan tombs. From what is known of the significance of mirrors in ancient times, they were not intended only for cosmetic use. In the language of the Egyptians and the Hittites, an ancient people of Asia Minor, the words for *mirror* and *life* were closely related. Some ancient peoples believed that mirrors had a power to cast spells over the soul, or to trap the soul of a dying person,

Hand mirror of polished bronze incised with mythological figures, palmette border.

if left uncovered in the presence of death. Although we don't know for certain that this was true of the Etruscans, the presence of so many mirrors in their tombs suggest that they believed mirrors had an important role to play in transporting the souls of the dead to the next world.

The jewels of the Etruscans were fabulous in workmanship and value. Their skilled craftsmen fashioned gold into exquisite bracelets, fibulae, diadems, necklaces and breastplates, earrings and finger rings. They knew the art of beating gold into paper-thin sheets from which they fashioned wreaths of leaves and flowers to adorn the hair. They mastered the techniques of filigree and granulation. In this latter art, gold was formed into tiny dots or grains which were applied by heat to fill in the area between other decorations on a flat or curved surface. Goldsmiths in ancient Mesopotamia, in Asia Minor, knew and practiced this art. The fact that the Etruscans alone among the Italic people were experts in this goldsmith's art is another clue that points to the possibility of an origin in Asia Minor.

Gold jewelry found in a tomb.
Fibulae in center, earrings, clasps.

Gold funerary wreath,
third century B.C.

Exquisite Etruscan necklace, sixth or fifth century B.C.
Gold-mounted glass beads alternating with pendants set
with glass. Part of a set of jewelry discovered at Vulci
about 1832.

In 1838, an Italian archpriest named Regolini and a general by the name of Galassi discovered near Ceveteri, in an area of tombs called the Sorbo, a tomb dating from the seventh century B.C. which evidently was the final resting place of royalty. It was found in the center of a tumulus with five graves surrounding it. These five had already been plundered of their contents, but the central tomb had escaped discovery. In it were two chambers connected by a long gallery, the lower walls of which were cut from solid rock. The upper part was built of stone blocks gradually overlapping each other to form a rough kind of vault. This was a primitive kind of construction used by early Mediterranean people from the Aegean to Sardinia in the west and indicates the great age of this tomb. It was not until the sixth century B.C., a hundred years later, that the Etruscans began to carve houses for their dead out of solid rock.

Perhaps the priest and the general, whose names have been given to this tomb, had the same shattering experience that others had when, after centuries of darkness, light first penetrated into the somber depths of the burial place. The richly clad silent figures of the dead seemed to be sleeping. A moment later, as the outside air reached them, they vanished into dust.

It was fortunate that this inner tomb had not been robbed or vandalized, for it contained some of the richest treasure found in Etruscan Italy. In the front chamber the body of a man rested on a bronze bed. In the chamber to the rear a woman lay on a stone couch. Both were

Long gallery of Regolini-Galassi Tomb, Cerveteri, seventh
century B.C. Note vaulted ceiling.

surrounded by rich gifts. The woman's name, Larthia, was inscribed on silver utensils placed beside her. The man is believed to have been her son whose death took place some time after his mother's. They each may have occupied the royal throne of Caere in turn.

In a niche near the entrance was an earthenware urn containing the ashes of a warrior, judging by the weapons near at hand and the charred remains of a two-wheeled war chariot with bronze fittings. Nearby in the vaulted gallery was a flat-bedded four-wheeled vehicle banded with copper which was used to transport the bodies to the tomb.

Larthia wore a large gold breastplate covered with incised designs of plants and animals. Her cloak was held together by a gold clasp in two sections, a masterpiece of the goldsmith's craft. The upper section is oval with five gold lions on it, surrounded by embossed lotus flowers. The hinged joint of woven gold mesh connects it with a smaller oval plate on which tiny golden ducklings parade across the curved surface. Between these vertically raised duckling figures are small embossed lions outlined with the tiny points of gold granulation which give them sheen and glitter.

Richly ornamented wide gold bracelets were on her arms and gold brooches and a necklace at her throat. All of these wondrous examples of Etruscan goldsmith's skill may be seen in the Gregorian Museum of the Vatican in Rome where the entire contents of the Regolini-Galassi tomb have been placed, including the restored chariot,

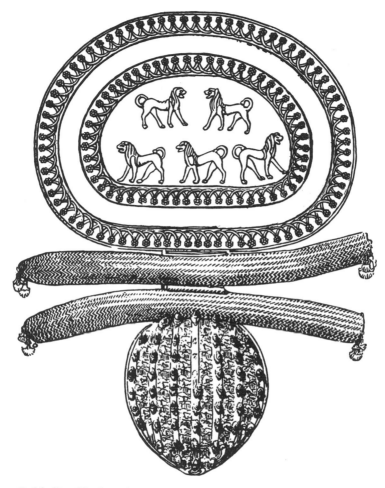

Gold disc fibula (pin or clasp) found in the Regolini-Galassi tomb near Cerveteri, from the first half of the seventh century B.C. Fine granulation outlines the lions in the upper shield and the seven rows of little ducklings in the lower shield.

the bronze bed, and enlarged photographs of the interior of the tomb.

Music, as the wall paintings indicate, played a vital part in Etruscan life. Aristotle is said to have remarked, "The Tyrrhenians fight, knead dough, and beat their slaves to the sound of the flute." Aelian, a Roman author of a later period, produced a long work, *On the Nature of Animals,* in which he wrote:

> We are told that the Tuscans not only catch deer and boars by means of nets and dogs, as is the normal custom in the field, but even more frequently by the aid of music. This is how they do it: On all sides they set out nets and other instruments of the chase to lay traps for the animals. A skillful flautist takes up position and plays the purest and

Etruscan youth playing the double flute, from Tomb of the Leopards, Tarquinia.

most harmonious melody. . . . When the sound comes to their ears, they are at first astonished and afraid, then they are overcome by the irresistible pleasure of the music and, transported, they forget their young and their lairs. . . . Animals do not like to go far from their homes. Yet, as if drawn by some charm, they are forced to approach and the power of the melody makes them fall into the nets, the victims of music.

Among the musical instruments the Etruscans played were the double pipes, the cithara, the lyre, a percussion instrument similar to castanets, horns—short or long and curling—and trumpets.

Dancing, too, was an essential aspect of Etruscan life. Wall paintings show women in lively round dances, weapon dances by men, and dance games of youths and maidens. There were guilds for dancers and musicians. As Rome grew in power the guilds were frequently summoned to that city to take part in ceremonies of atonement or in homage to the gods.

We know this from the writings of Livy, the Roman historian who wrote a history of the Roman people in many volumes. In one of them he describes such an occasion which took place in 364 B.C. when the Etruscan world was already beginning its decline. It is interesting to realize that the Romans, even though they resented, distrusted, and sometimes feared the Etruscans, still thought highly enough of their skills in music and the dance to invite them to perform on sacred occasions.

VII

Etruscan Ships
and Greek Vases

In the eighth century B.C., when the Etruscans were already well established in west central Italy, the Greek city-states, in need of new sources of raw materials, sent colonists to southern Italy and west to Sicily, to establish trading centers. Overpopulation and lack of food, as well as the urge to adventure and the lure of greener pastures over the far horizon, encouraged emigration from Greece. Settlements along the south coast of Italy's boot included Tarentum (present-day Taranto), Sybaris, Crotona, and Locri. The native tribes were friendly to the Greeks and what started out as trading posts prospered and became powerful cities.

Greek colonies on the nearby island of Sicily fared less well at first, for they found themselves in constant conflict with the Phoenicians who came from Carthage, on the north coast of Africa.

At this time, the northernmost Greek colony in Italy was Cumae, located on a volcanic height just west of present-day Naples. Further south, below the gulf of Salerno, a colony was established by the wealthy town of Sybaris. It was called Poseidonia, after the sea god Poseidon. The Sybarites then pioneered a route through the mountains to Poseidonia from their own city on the gulf of Taranto so that goods brought by Etruscan ships to Poseidonia could be transported on muleback to Sybaris. Sybarite and Etruscan ships were thus spared from attacks by Carthaginian pirates and from the perils of the straits between Italy and Sicily where dread currents and whirlpools claimed many ships. In greater safety the Etruscan imports could be sent by sea from Sybaris to homeland Greece.

At Paestum, as Poseidonia is called today, the skeletal roofless ruins of magnificent Greek temples still stand on the wide plain between blue mountains and the sea. They mutely speak of the glory that was Magna Graecia, Greater Greece. Sybaris itself, famed in the ancient world for its self-indulgent luxury, was utterly destroyed by its envious neighbor city Crotona in 510 B.C. Not a vestige of it remained above ground. It was not until 1968, after years of search, that the buried foundations of this ancient city were discovered.

Etruscan ships brought their ore and grain to Poseidonia and traded them for wine, oil, spices, and decorated vases and jugs, products of skilled Greek craftsmen, that had been brought by ship to Sybaris from Corinth and Athens in Greece and Miletus in Asia Minor. The number of Greek vases and utensils of many kinds which have been rescued from Etruscan tombs speak of this thriving trade. Some of the greatest examples of the Greek potters' art would have been lost if the Etruscans had not buried so many of them with their dead.

During the sixth and fifth centuries B.C., engraved Etruscan mirrors, bronze candlesticks, weapons, and vessels of bronze and other precious metals, as well as fine Etruscan woolens, were in demand by other Mediterranean countries in trade. Sandals with copper nails fastening the soles and with gold and silver straps were much prized by the ladies of Greece.

Etruria herself was one of the biggest markets for pottery from Athens and Corinth. Potters from Greece, like Aristonothos, even found their way to Etruscan cities and set up shop there. Aristonothos had studied with master potters in the ceramics section of Athens, then emigrated to the west. For a time he worked in Sicily, but eventually moved on to Cerveteri where he established his own pottery.

It was the custom for artists to inscribe their names on works of ceramic art that they had created. One marvelous sample bearing the name of Aristonothos survives. Found in Cerveteri, and now displayed with other early pottery in the Palace of the Conservators on the Capitoline Hill in Rome, it is a large earthenware bowl for mixing wine and water called a *krater*. The damaged base has been pieced together. A double row of large

Greek red-figured vases found in Etruscan tombs.

The Aristonothos krater or mixing bowl, mid-seventh century B.C., found in Cerveteri.

black checks forms a band around the lower area of the krater, while above—between the two curved handles— are scenes of a naval battle on one side, on the other the figure of Odysseus with his four companions in the act of thrusting a heated spear into the eye of the Cyclops, Polyphemus.

The influence of Greece was everywhere apparent in Etruscan art and customs. But the Etruscans infused their own individual character into whatever they borrowed from the Greeks, adapting and modifying and making it their own. The Greeks clung to the philosophical idea of the beautiful, purifying and idealizing the human figure, while the Etruscan sculptors sought realism in their work, even to the extent of exaggerating some feature of the subject, as in a caricature, if it increased likeness to life.

Etruscan pottery was often modeled after the shapes of Greek vases, and the individual pieces are called today by Greek names. Since each pot or vase served a particular purpose, shapes came to be standardized according to function.

An enormous two-handled jar, the *pithos,* with either a wide or narrow mouth, was used to store wine, oil, or grain. Another storage jar, the *stamnos,* had a squat oval body. Wine was stored at home in an *amphora,* a tall two-handled jar with painted decorations. Amphoras used for shipping wine overseas had pointed bottoms so they could be propped against a wall with ease. At home the wine from an amphora was poured into a *krater* where it was mixed with water from a wide-mouthed jug called a *hydria* which had three handles.

The *oinochoe* was a small pitcher which servants dipped into the krater to fill their masters' drinking cups —the *skyphos,* a deep two-handled cup on a flat base, or the *kylix,* which was wider and shallower with a stem joining it to a footed base and handles extending out on either side.

Libations or offerings of oil were poured from a *leky-thos,* a tall slender pitcher with one handle. Fragrant ointments, oils, or perfumes were stored in a small jar called an *aryballos* or an *alabastron,* depending on the shape. Toilet articles and jewelry were kept in a cylindrical box called a *cista,* which could be also made of bronze.

Silhouettes of Etruscan pottery modeled after Greek vessels and called by Greek names.

Column Krater   Amphora   Stamnos   Hydria

Aryballos   Kylix   Pyxis   Lekythos   Skyphos   Oinochoe

The color of the finished pottery was determined by the kind of clay used and the length of the firing. Black designs or figures against a red clay background were achieved by applying very fine liquid clay or "slip" to the surface of a vase in a design or pattern which turned black in the firing process, producing the "black-figured ware." At other times the background was filled in with slip, leaving the figures to come out red against black. The artist could then paint any amount of detail onto the red figures with slip which would show black against red when fired.

The early decorations for pottery were in the Geometric Style: checks, zigzags, circles, and later a wavering line called a *meander,* a word still used when describing a wandering or meandering brook.

Later the various kinds of vases were painted with lively scenes of chariot races, battles, or gods and goddesses.

Black bucchero ware, Narce, eighth or seventh century B.C.

The Etruscans

The Etruscans developed a gleaming black polished pottery, called by the Italians *bucchero* ware, which was entirely their own. It was heavily ornamented and decorated, sometimes with incised designs, other times with figures, human and animal, which were added to the basic clay shapes. Specimens have been found in Sardinia, Corsica, North Africa, Greece, southern France and Spain, which indicates how far afield the Etruscan trade extended.

Black bucchero vases with animal decorations, seventh century B.C.

VIII

The Indestructible Bond

Religion was the indestructible bond that united the Etruscans. Every year people from all over Etruria thronged to the sacred grove of the god Vultumna in the territory of Volsinii for the religious rites that were celebrated there. The Etruscans took part in games and pageants, prize fights and acrobatics, and enjoyed the displays of tempting and beautiful articles at the fair which was held at the same time.

The driving of the year-nail into the shrine of Nortia, goddess of Fortune, to mark the end of another year was an important ceremony. The Etruscans believed that the lives of both individuals and nations were divided into periods of already determined lengths. Just as the different ages in a man's life are milestones on his way to death, so nations are born, come into their prime, and then make the downhill slide to oblivion. The Etruscan priests and augurs predicted that there would be eight or at the most ten of these periods, now known as *seculae,* and afterwards the Etruscans would disappear as a race.

The signs of the gods foretold that the year 88 B.C. would be the beginning of their end. It is a strange fulfillment of this prophecy that the Etruscans' disappearance as a cultural and historical entity began at the end of the ninth *seculum* when they were submerged and engulfed by the Roman Empire.

Not surprisingly, therefore, the Etruscans were fatalistic about life and believed there was little they as a nation or as individuals could do to alter what fate had in store for them.

Their lives were governed by the rules laid down in the Disciplina Etrusca, revealed by the child-god Tages, a grandson of Tinia, the greatest of their gods. Tages was plowed out of the earth by a peasant named Tarchon who was terrified to have a goblinlike child with an old face and gray hair spring up from the furrow his plow had opened.

This strange apparition, according to legend, is supposed to have chanted the rules to the *lucumones,* the priest-kings, who gathered round and carefully recorded them. These rules regulated every aspect of Etruscan life. Procedures were given for the founding of cities, the distribution of land, the establishment of shrines. There were regulations for ritual sacrifices, prayers, and foretelling the future. Exact instructions were laid down for the burial of the dead, and for determining the will of

ETRUSCAN GODS AND THEIR COUNTERPARTS IN ROMAN AND GREEK MYTHOLOGY

ETRUSCAN	GREEK	ROMAN
The Major Gods		
TINIA, lord of the thunderbolts	ZEUS	JUPITER
UNI, his wife	HERA	JUNO
MENRVA, goddess of wisdom and the arts	ATHENA	MINERVA

These three formed a trinity which was introduced to Rome by the Etruscan kings.

ETRUSCAN	GREEK	ROMAN
The Lesser Gods		
NETHUNS, god of the sea, to whom the Etruscans felt particular devotion	POSEIDON	NEPTUNE
MARIS, god of war, who became lover of the goddess of love	ARES	MARS
TURAN, goddess of love	APHRODITE	VENUS
FUFLUNS, god of grape and ivy	DIONYSUS	
TURMS, god connected with funerary rites who guides souls to Hades	HERMES	MERCURY
SETHLAN, VELCHAN, gods of fire who throw thunderbolts and are patrons of smiths	HEPHAISTOS	VULCAN
HERCLE, god who symbolized strength, martial valor; also powerful god of water, springs, and the sea	HERAKLES	HERCULES

Gods Who Were Purely Etruscan
NORTIA, goddess of fortune who symbolized the irrevocable passage of time
MANTUS, god of death
VOLTUMNA, god of the sacred grove where the Twelve Cities held their annual meetings. He was taken over by the Romans as VERTUMNUS, god of plant life.

the gods from the shapes of livers of sacrificed animals, from the examination of their entrails, from the direction of the sound of thunder and flashes of lightning, and from the flight of birds. Tages himself was never seen again.

A special order of men was required to interpret the signs from the gods. They were called *haruspices* and were greatly honored. They were consulted before any important undertaking. The skilled haruspex who could interpret omens correctly had a greater influence than a king or a general.

Models of livers have been found, some in terra cotta, but the most notable one in bronze was discovered in 1877 near Piacenza, Italy. Quite possibly it was used to instruct beginner haruspices in the art of divining. Its outer or convex side was divided into compartments inscribed with the names of the Tuscan gods who occupied areas in the sky which were duplicated in the markings on the liver. Thus by studying the conformation of each area of an actual liver, the haruspex could determine the wishes of the god whose home was in the corresponding area of the heavens.

The founding of an Etruscan town was never haphazard. One might almost say that the Etruscans were among the first town planners. If the omens were favorable, the haruspices gave their approval to the site selected, which had to be on the summit of a hill. The founder of the town then followed the sacred ritual. Plutarch, a Greek biographer of the first century A.D., reports that when Romulus was ready to found Rome "he sent for men from Tuscany who prescribed all the details in accordance with certain sacred ordinances."

The founder was required to yoke a white bull and a white cow to his plow, the bull on the right, the cow on the left. The plowshare had to be of bronze. Then he plowed a furrow counterclockwise, following the contours of the land but keeping the area to be enclosed as nearly rectangular as possible. The men who followed after threw the earth clods inwards to mark the line of the future wall. "Where they proposed to put a gate, there they took the share out of the ground," Plutarch tells us, "lifted the plow over and left a vacant space." All of the wall would be considered sacred except the gates. If the gates, too, were held to be sacred according to the ritual followed, it would have been impossible to bring things necessary, but considered unclean, into or out of the city.

The town would then be laid out according to an exact geometrical formula with a thick defensive wall. The main gate always faced south. From this a broad straight road ran northward to the highest ground where the main temple would be built. The north wall, unlike those of Roman cities, had no gate, but the east and west walls each had one and were connected by another straight road which crossed the first at right angles. On either side of the east-west road, depending on the size of the town, there would be other streets. Each gate was topped by a massive arch decorated with sculptures and reliefs. One such has survived at Perugia, another at Volterra.

Special attention was given to water supply and drainage. Along the streets were ditches, often cut out of solid rock and covered over with flat slabs of stone, which carried off waste water.

The finished city crowned a rocky height which dropped steeply away on every side with water flowing around it in natural ravines. Beyond lay the city of the dead which the living could see from their dwellings on the summit.

A town might have several sanctuaries, each dedicated to a different god, but the major temple was always built on the highest spot. Descriptions of temples are given by the Roman architect Vetruvius who lived in the reign of Emperor Augustus (27 B.C.–A.D. 14). He describes them as wide squat buildings constructed of perishable wood or brick, placed on stone platforms. Platforms with foundations have been uncovered which reveal the floor plan. A temple consisted of three rooms where the images of the gods were kept. The central room or *cela* was flanked on either side by the smaller rooms. Two double rows of four columns supported the tiled roof of the portico or porch. The triangular pediment above the columns was covered with terra cotta ornaments and the ends of the roof-tile joints were hidden by terra cotta antefixes. These could be masks of gods and goddesses and lesser deities, demons, satyrs, or the snake-haired Medusa. They were usually placed in the center of a fluted shell-

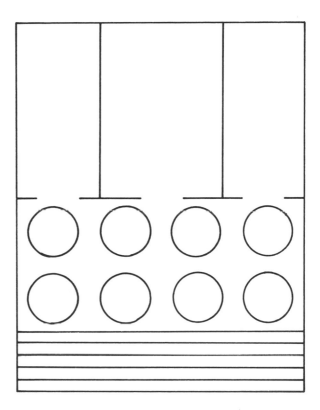

Floor plan of an Etruscan temple. Steps leading up to the portico, with double row of four columns supporting portico roof. Each of the three rooms was the shrine of a god.

like terra cotta frame and were perhaps intended to discourage evil spirits. Sometimes, as at the temple in Veii, life-sized figures were placed along the ridgepole of the roof. All were painted in gay bright colors that must have shone brilliantly under the clear Etruscan skies.

Neither Etruscan houses nor temples survived the ravages of conquest and of time. The rock-cut tombs and some cinerary urns shaped like houses give an idea of how Etruscan houses looked. We know that they were built around a central court with rooms opening from it, called by the Romans an *atrium*. The Romans adopted this form of architecture. Many similar houses have been preserved in the ruins of Pompeii and Herculaneum, just south of Naples, which were engulfed by a smothering blanket of lava and ashes that poured down from the erupting volcano Vesuvius in A.D. 79. Roman writers refer to the *atrium tuscanicum,* giving credit to the Etruscans for one style of atrium.

Nenfro lion which once guarded the entrance to a tomb.

IX
Another Mystery:
Why Did They Vanish?

In a book called *The Art of Etruria and Early Rome,* the author, G. A. Mansuelli, states: "There is scarcely a voice in Roman literature that does not speak of Etruria with the greatest respect. . . . Etruria, in the tradition of the ancients, appears . . . as a teacher of civilization to the Italic peoples, and particularly to the Romans."

Why, then, does the mute language of Etruscan art alone survive to speak of Etruria's once great role in Italian history and of the tragedy which overtook her people? Here is another mystery, but there are clues to the cause of her downfall.

Although there is disagreement among scholars as to exact dates, we may assume that the ninth and eighth centuries B.C. saw the beginnings of Etruscan civilization. As Livy has told us, Etruria's power and influence eventually reached from the plains of the Po in the north to

Campania, a province in the south. The confederation of city-states in the north had as its capital Mantua, named for Mantus, god of the dead. Years later, in the first century B.C., Mantua was to become famous as the birthplace of Virgil, author of *The Aeneid,* the great Latin epic poem about the origins of Rome. It is probable that Etruscan blood flowed in his veins. Included in this territory were the towns of Hadria and Spina, located near the mouth of the Po which were established by the Etruscans for trade with the savage countries farther north in Switzerland and Burgundy.

South of Rome, in the pleasant region known as Campania, yet another confederation of towns had been established. Its chief city was Capua. Evidence has come to light in recent years which indicates that Herculaneum and Pompeii were also Etruscan at that time. Sorrento, too, on its commanding headland overlooking the Bay of Naples, was believed to have been a member of the southern confederation.

Only the Greek city Cumae, west of Naples, stood between central Etruria and her colonies in Campania. During all this time the Umbrians, east of the River Tiber, successfully withstood Etruscan penetration and thwarted her almost complete domination of Italy.

During the fifth century, the period of greatest Etruscan power, Etruscan ships commanded the Tyrrhenian Sea; the offshore island of Elba with its wealth of minerals belonged to Etruria; she had colonies on Corsica, and

ITALY AT THE HEIGHT OF ETRUSCAN POWER

SPHERES OF INFLUENCE: ETRUSCAN

CARTHAGINIAN

GREEK

TO R.
Mantua
Adria
Spina
Felsina
Ravenna
Fiesole
Rimini
Pisa
Arezzo
Cortona
ELBA
Populonia
Perugia
Chiusi
Vetulonia
Rusellae
Volsinii
Vulci
Tarquinii
Veii
Caere
Rome
Praeneste
Capua
Cumae
Naples
Poseidonia
CORSICA
SARDINIA
Taranto
Sybaris
Crotona
Locri
Reggio
Carthage
Syracuse
AFRICA
SICILY

there was an Etruscan presence on Sardinia until the Carthaginians took over control of that large island.

Greek colonization in southern Italy had begun in the eighth century B.C. The Greeks were content to limit their settlements to coastal areas and did not penetrate inland. Eventually they pushed their way to the eastern shore of Spain and to southern France. Antibes, Nice, and Marseille were Greek settlements. Their first effort to colonize Corsica was repulsed after a sea battle with the Etruscans aided by Carthage, the powerful city on the African coast which warred frequently with the Greek colonies. But in 478 B.C. the Etruscan navy was decisively defeated by the Greeks at Cumae, a disaster from which it never recovered.

Etruria began to feel threatened by Greek expansion and by the growing power of Rome. At the end of the sixth century the last Tarquin king, Tarquinius Superbus, was forced out of Rome by a people who had grown resentful of his tyrannical ways. After nearly a hundred years of rule by Etruscan kings, Rome became a republic with an elected Senate. She was constantly at war with her neighbors and grew rich on the booty she acquired, in new lands and captive people who became her slaves.

As Rome grew in power, she turned her attention to the rich and seemingly impregnable Etruscan city of Veii a few miles to the north. There had been friction between the two cities with attacks by first one and then the other. At last the Roman general Marcus Furius Camillus made a concentrated effort to overthrow Veii. His soldiers began a siege which lasted for ten years. It ended in 396 B.C. when he succeeded in penetrating the fortified walls of Veii by the ingenious means of sending his forces through an underground tunnel into the center of the city and taking it by surprise. The inhabitants were slaughtered or taken captive to become slaves, the buildings burned, and the sacred statue of the Goddess Uni removed from the temple and carried off in triumph to Rome, to be renamed Juno. During these ten years of danger and peril none of Veii's sister cities came to her aid. Her fall was a mortal blow to Etruscan power.

Early in the fourth century B.C., the cities of the north fell before the onslaught of invading barbaric tribes from western Europe, known as Gauls, who crossed the Alps and poured down into Italy. They swept southward, pillaging and burning, overrunning all of Etruria in time, though the stoutly walled hill towns of central Etruria resisted successfully. But crops were destroyed, fields laid waste.

A second invasion by these Gauls in 390 B.C. swept all the way to Rome which was captured and sacked. Livy describes how "the wild songs and discordant shouts filled the air with hideous noise," and how the Roman army fled before these savage barbarians. They were huge men who went into battle half naked and preferred hand-to-hand combat to fighting in orderly ranks as was the Roman custom. General Camillus, who had been appointed dictator by the Roman Senate, finally was able to drive them out of the country. In a classic example of locking the barn door after the horse was stolen, he ordered a new and stronger defensive wall built around Rome.

At about the same time the Etruscans were dealt another blow when the southern group of cities in Campania were overrun by warlike mountain tribes, the Samnites, who coveted the rich coastal cities and the pleasing climate of Campania, and the islands of Elba and Corsica were lost to the Greeks from Sicily. This succession of catastrophes signaled the end of the Etruscan empire. Only the birthplace of Etruscan civilization, Tuscany, remained.

What would have happened, one cannot help but wonder, if the Etruscan cities had submerged their own local interests and loyalties for the greater good of Etruria as a whole? United, could they have withstood the pressure of Rome? We shall never know.

Instead Rome was able to lop them off one by one. Cerveteri, only twenty-five miles from Rome, saw her danger. Rather than suffer the fate of Veii, she resigned from the Etruscan confederation and cast her lot with the victorious power. Rome allowed her to keep a measure of self-government.

Tarquinia was compelled to deed to Rome a large part of her territory. Later, when the Etruscans made a brief alliance with their former enemies the Gauls, to proceed against Rome, they were jointly defeated in bloody battles before the walls of Arezzo and at Lake Vadimon, midway between Orvieto and Rome, in 283 B.C. After that, Vulci and Volsinii were forced to sign treaties of peace on Rome's terms. They were severe. Vulci was compelled to hand over a large part of its territory, and in 273 B.C. Rome founded a colony there—Cosa, high above the sea. Little remains today of this once thriving Roman town. White oxen graze among the olive trees which have grown up between the foundation stones and ruined walls. From the acropolis, the gaunt shattered remains of a Roman temple still look down on the shining Tyrrhenian Sea.

A revolt of slaves led to the downfall of the powerful city of Volsinii. Rome granted citizenship to her freed slaves who could then exercise their own abilities to shape their futures. But in Etruscan society, there was no crossing of social barriers between the ruling class, the common people, and the slaves. Those at the foot of the social ladder had no hope of moving upward.

When the slaves in Volsinii turned against their masters, an appeal for aid was made to Rome, the only power the threatened rulers could look to for help, as their sister cities had already fallen to Rome and were both indifferent to their plight and powerless. A worse mistake could not have been made. Roman legions moved on Volsinii, but instead of putting down the revolt, they attacked the city, looted and killed, and destroyed houses and monuments. The few persons who survived were moved nearer to Lake Bolsena where Rome built a new town, the Bolsena of today.

After all of Etruria had become subject to Rome, she

still managed to keep her own individuality and traditions until just before the Christian Era. Her workshops continued to turn out many fine products and works of art. Only the towns nearest Rome lost their prosperity. The cities to the north—Chiusi, Perugia, Cortona, Arezzo, and Volterra—continued to enjoy a measure of industrial and commercial wealth.

In the first century B.C., some of these northern cities made the fatal error of siding with the Roman general, Marius, against his rival, General Sulla. These two men were in violent conflict with one another. Sulla, the victor, avenged himself against the Etruscans by planting military colonies within the towns and devastating the countryside. This was the end. From that time on, Etruria had no vestige of independence. The once proud Etruscan civilization became a fading memory.

The lack of political unity which kept the city-states from aiding one another when danger threatened from outside, the rigidity of social structure which caused dissatisfaction and finally revolt among slaves, the fatalism of the Etruscan religion which made the nation impotent to change what seemed ordained, and the love of luxury which may have weakened the moral fiber of the leaders of the people—these are the probable basic causes for the downfall of the Etruscan nation.

X

The Painted Tombs
of Tarquinia

The present-day town of Tarquinia was known as Corneto until the last century, when it was given the old-time Etruscan name. It is situated on a high ridge of land, the hill of the necropolis of the old city. Its tall towers, ancient rooftops, and churches look out over a wide plain where thousands of Etruscan tombs lie below the grassy surface, with the sea gleaming in the distance.

Beyond, across a dipping hollow, green corn grows in rows among the fallen stones and blocks of masonry from the vanished walls of what was once the first city of all Etruria. After its loss of power to Rome, the original Tarquinia had gradually declined, becoming more obscure and neglected as the centuries unrolled, beset by famine, poverty, and war until it was finally abandoned to the thrust of root and vine and eventually to the plow.

Corneto, which grew up nearby with a history going

back to A.D. 504, was renamed Tarquinia in 1872. It is the starting point for visiting the most notable, in number and distinction, of the painted Etruscan tombs. Its magnificent museum, housed in a former palace, the Palazzo Vitelleschi, contains many Etruscan treasures.

One enters the museum through a colonnaded courtyard overlooked by open galleries and Gothic arches. A square tower rises from one corner containing shallow steps which zigzag upward to the floor above, where five wall paintings rescued from tombs may be seen. Against the wall on one landing of these wide sloping stairs is a pair of spirited winged horses, among the greatest of the ancient world, with traces of color still remaining on the honey-colored terra cotta. Harnessed to a chariot, they once graced the pediment of a Tarquinian temple about 300 B.C.

The courtyard and lower floor contain sarcophagi of rough-hewn nenfro, a local stone, with carved stone figures reclining on their elbows and looking up from the coffin lids. In the showcases are many amphoras, hydrias, black and red figured vases, pieces of bucchero ware, votive offerings in bronze, spears, shields, helmets, and cinerary urns.

But the glory of the museum are the five reconstructed tombs on the top floor. The tomb paintings, painstakingly detached from the walls, have been affixed to canvas, carefully restored, and placed in relationship to each other as they were found in the real tombs. Here they no longer are endangered by the ruinous effect of dampness seeping through the ground and sudden changes of temperature. The visitor may study them in comfort and revel in their vitality and beauty.

The earliest Tarquinian tomb, the Tomb of the Bulls (mid-sixth century B.C.) is here with its paintings of the naked Troilus on his high-stepping blue-maned horse, the armored figure of Achilles hiding behind a fountain as though waiting to attack, and the two man-faced bulls from which the tomb takes its name.

Here also is the Tomb of the Chariots (490 B.C.) with its frieze of naked athletes riding, jumping, wrestling, pole-vaulting, throwing the javelin, or readying their high-necked horses for the chariot races.

The Tomb of the Triclinium (about 470 B.C.) is per-

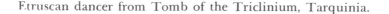

Etruscan dancer from Tomb of the Triclinium, Tarquinia.

haps the most famous of the tombs in Tarquinia, and it also may be seen in the museum. *Triclinium* is the Latin name for a couch extending around three sides of a room, where diners recline to eat from low tables. Hence this tomb is also known as the Tomb of the Feast. Brilliant colors highlight the figures of the women on the side walls with their richly banded garments swinging to the movement of the dance, their limbs glimpsed through the transparent tunics, and three couples at the banquet tables. Trees delicately traced between the dancers have strange birds perched on their branches. Two musicians move to their own silent music. It is with joy the Etruscans honor their dead.

A lapse of sixty years occurred between the discovery of the Tomb of the Bulls, using modern scientific methods, and the discovery of the Tomb of the Olympics in 1958 (see photos on pages 94–95). The paintings of lively

Six of the twelve photographic drill shots from the Tomb of the Olympics, sixth century B.C. The other six were of greatly damaged sections of the fresco.

sports scenes for which the tomb is named—some badly damaged—have been removed from its walls and can now be seen in the Tarquinia Museum. This tomb dates from the late sixth century B.C.

The two other museum tombs are the Tomb of the Ship, named after a two-masted vessel with sailors working on her (mid-fifth century B.C.), and the Tomb of the Funeral Bed.

From the museum a bus with a guide carries one to the wide treeless plain beyond the town where lies the city of the dead, dotted with small slant-roofed buildings which are the covered entrances to the tombs. Each has a side doorway which the guide unlocks. He switches on a light and conducts the visitor down a steep iron staircase into the tomb where wall paintings spring to life at the touch of the electric switch, their colors still vibrant and glowing after more than twenty-five hundred years.

The artists who did the paintings had to work by the light of flaming torches. First the rock walls of the tombs had to be covered with a thin layer of plaster. Only pigments which would retain their color when painted on lime mortar could be used: bright primary colors—reds, blues, yellows—which had to be laid on swiftly while the plaster was wet. The painter was forced to consider the effect of the darkness of the tomb on color and tone and the fact that the paintings could be seen only by torchlight. The dead for whom they were painted presumably needed no light, but the family who first commissioned the work must have had to approve it before they themselves took up their last residence in eternal darkness. Only nobility, the ruling classes, priests, and the military castes were laid to rest in these chambered tombs. Lesser folk were accommodated in simpler burial places.

Christopher Hampton, a young English poet, has written a fascinating account of his visit to Etruria called *Etruscan Survival,* published in 1970. He describes vividly the paintings in many of the most notable tombs in Tarquinia. "The symbolic images which decorate the tombs," he writes, "the curves and rippling lines, the circlets and flowers and leaves, the leaping dolphins and sea horses, the birds and leopards and lions and bulls are . . . done with swift unhesitant conviction, just as men might speak the language they were born to speak. Even the occasional hesitations that occur are rather like the momentary hesitations and wrong directions that people take when they are speaking passionately . . . and it is so with these paintings; they are done with a 'childlike' intentness of feeling, a passionate absorption that enacts and presents the forms without comment and without reflection."

Indeed, the viewer is made to feel the same sense of awe that the Etruscans must have felt over the mystery of the journey out of life into death.

One of the most memorable tombs in the necropolis is the Tomb of Hunting and Fishing (about 500 B.C.). Here are birds and dolphins leaping and diving, a little man fishing from a boat, another man diving from a rock. The men wear tunics as blue as the birds soaring above them in the sky; their skin is red, they are quick with life.

Other tombs are the Tomb of the Augurs, the Tomb of the Baron, the Tomb of the Lionesses, the Tomb of the Leopards, the Tomb of the Shields, and the Tomb of the Orcus (a classical god of the Underworld). This one lies under the modern cemetery of Tarquinia. Both of these last two tombs date from the end of the third century B.C., and they reveal a noticeable change in the Etruscan spirit. Instead of the former joyousness and acceptance of death as a natural entry into another happy

Tomb of the Leopards, Tarquinia.
Men and women banqueting together.

Banqueting couple in Tomb of the Shields, painted at the time Tarquinia first came under Roman rule. "The spirit, the zest, the vitality and joy seem to have gone."

world, these tomb paintings are characterized by gloomy foreboding.

The tombs themselves are unusually large. On the walls of the Tomb of the Shields a half-obliterated winged figure hovers. In the large room of the fourteen shields, the banqueting couple and all of the details have little emotional impact. The spirit, the zest, the vitality and joy seem to have gone out of them. When we realize that this tomb was painted at the time Tarquinia first came under Roman rule, becoming an unwilling subject state, we begin to understand.

This change in the Etruscan soul is even more apparent in the Tomb of the Orcus. Here the Etruscans seem to have become obsessed with the harrowing details of the journey into Hades. Vividly depicted are the horrors of the world beyond the grave, peopled with demons and monsters and weird writhing serpents. Viewing them from a banqueting table are a man and woman reclining side by side on a couch. Most of the lady's figure has crumbled away; only the head remains. It is an unforgettable portrait of a young woman whose name was Velia, according to the inscription. Her husband's head and figure have been largely effaced, but the bearing and dress of Velia indicate that she was of gentle birth. Myrtle and laurel leaves crown her auburn hair which hangs loose in curls over her temples and ears. Her pure delicate profile stands out radiantly against the ominous background. But sadness is suggested by her down-turned lips.

These tombs tells us more than mere words could of the unhappy fate that had overtaken this once joyous people. That is their great value.

Another remarkable aspect of the Tarquinian tomb painting is the absence of any hint of warfare, though we know that the Etruscans were often engaged in battles. Here the dead are honored and entertained by dancers

Velia, head of young woman
from the Tomb of the Orcus.

who seem to sway and step to the lilt of the double flute,
lifting their long-fingered hands to its cadences. Their
faces smile their mysterious smiles, the athletes perform
in friendly competition. The feasts spread before the
banqueters are offerings which speak to them of the love
and respect in which they are held.

Although many centuries passed while the Etruscan
frescoes lay buried in the dark of tombs, it is difficult to
believe that the creative spirit implicit in them did not
ferment like yeast and rise again to flower in the great
Tuscan artists—Michelangelo, Leonardo da Vinci,
Giotto—of medieval and Renaissance Italy.

XI
Science's Sixth Sense

Many of the tombs in Tarquinia have been discovered and opened since 1955 through the efforts of the Lerici Foundation of the Milan Polytechnical School. Founded by Carlo M. Lerici, a retired engineer who amassed a great fortune in stainless steel, the foundation has been in the forefront of archaeological prospecting using new scientific tools which give man the sixth sense of seeing underground.

Carlo Lerici had moved to Rome after retirement seeking a more comfortable climate than northern Italy provided. How he became interested in the Etruscans is a story in itself. Planning a future tomb for himself and his wife, he was casting around for ideas of how to embellish it. A friend suggested he visit the Villa Giulia, a museum at the north entrance to Rome's Borghese Gardens which houses a vast collection of Etruscan art as well as many sculptured sarcophagi bearing the effigies of long-dead Etruscans.

There he saw one which had enormous appeal for him. In softly colored terra cotta it portrays a husband and wife posed as though at a banqueting table. The husband rests on one elbow, his other arm thrown tenderly around his wife who leans against him. Her face is lit with a serene smile, her hands raised palm up in a welcoming gesture to death. Her hair, bound into small twisted strands, falls over her shoulders. Her husband's

The Married Couple, polychrome terra cotta sarcophagus from Cerveteri, sixth century B.C., which aroused Carlo Lerici's interest in the Etruscans.

head is turned slightly toward her. He has a small pointed beard; his hair is plaited and lies in a straight line across his back. They have a wide-eyed look of acceptance. Their attitude is one of trust and affection.

Carlo Lerici was so impressed with this beautiful representation of conjugal love that he had it copied in bronze for his and his wife's future burial place. Meanwhile, through his fascination with the other treasures in the Villa Giulia, he had caught Etruscan fever, the desire to know more about this mysterious people. The only way to satisfy this wish was to search for tombs which had not yet been vandalized, in the hope that they would provide new clues to the mystery of Etruscan origins and language.

In the course of building his fortune, Lerici had become interested in geophysics, especially the new electronic devices that can probe the earth for valuable metals. In its search for tombs, the Lerici Foundation began to use an instrument called a proton-magnetometer which had been developed for archaeological prospecting by the Research Laboratory for Archaeology and Art History at Oxford University in England. It can detect solid objects beneath the earth's surface by returning electrical impulses which are read by a computer. This instrument was used most successfully in locating the buried walls of ancient Sybaris.

The first step in the new search for Etruscan tombs was to make aerial photographic surveys over the vast areas of Etruria. Photographic enlargements of the contours of the land and the pattern of vegetation revealed the possible location of many tombs. One telltale clue was the lighter color of vegetation and its relative thinness where a tomb existed underground. This enables the prospector to choose likely sites for electrical surveys with the proton-magnetometer which pinpoints the exact locations of tombs.

An electric drill pierces the earth and rock and bores a hole in the roof of the tomb located by the magnetome-

The photographic-electric drill.

ter. To "see underground" a small electrically operated camera with a flash attachment, developed by the foundation's laboratory, is used. It is inserted into a metal cylinder with a window at the lower end. This periscope-in-reverse can be extended up to twenty feet in length. It in turn is fitted into the hole in the tomb roof and rotated so that the camera, by remote control, can scan the entire inner perimeter of the tomb walls. The twelve resulting pictures reveal whether the tomb has painted frescoes, whether it has been looted by thieves, and, if not, what the contents are and where the entrance corridor is placed. This tells the prospector where to begin digging and saves an enormous amount of time and energy.

In 1954 a meeting took place in Italy between archaeologists and engineers from several countries to consider how aerial and geophysical prospecting could be applied to archaeological exploration. Among those attending were the superintendents of antiquities from the various regions of Italy, representatives from the American Academy and the British and Swedish schools and institutes in Rome, and scholars in fine arts and applied geophysics.

The real search for tombs got under way the following year. The first experimental survey was made at Cerveteri, and the systematic exploration of Monte Abbetone, one of the three necropolises there, was begun by the Milan Polytechnical School financed by the Lerici Foundation. For centuries these three burial places have been a main center for clandestine digging and one of the major sources for illicit trading in objects stolen from ex-

The periscope.

cavations. The tomb robbers, called *tombaroli,* sell their loot to dealers who smuggle the finds to distribution centers abroad. There the Etruscan antiquities are sold to private collectors or to museums in America and Europe.

During the time the team of experts worked in the Monte Abbetone, they located 650 tombs from which 10,000 objects were taken, many of them restored at Foundation expense, and sent on to museums in Italy. The first tomb opened, Tomb 4, dates back to the late seventh century B.C. It was a mound tomb entered through a narrow corridor called a *dromos*. Large clay storage jars (pithoi), some of them still containing flour, were found. Other objects were earthenware vases decorated with birds, a Corinthian skyphos (drinking cup), and many fine black bucchero vases.

Other tombs contained amphoras. One held the ashes of a dead man and fragments of ivory; there were sepulchral urns and red- and black-figured Attic vases. In Tomb 304 a bucchero oinochoe (pitcher) decorated with animal engravings and a long Etruscan inscription was discovered.

Tomb 610 contained three chambers, the doors and windows framed with molded reliefs. When opened it was filled to the ceiling with water and mud, the water having apparently seeped in from some underground source. The water had to be pumped out through the bore hole. To empty one chamber required two full

Pictures of the interior of a tomb taken by

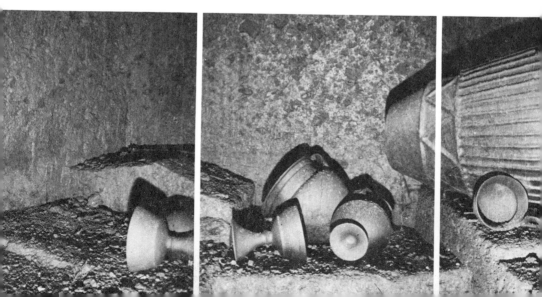

days. Then began the careful slow work of prying loose the objects it contained from the hardened mud, but what a treasure was revealed when the objects were cleaned and examined!

There were many clay, bucchero, and earthenware vases as well as twenty-seven Greek black- and red-figured vases. The most noteworthy was a large black-figured amphora decorated on one side with the image of Dionysus, the wine god, and satyrs picking grapes (see photo on page 17), on the other with maidens bathing in a pool. Experts believe these drawings to be the work of a noted artist known as "The Master of Priam." Priam was the famous king of Troy, the city-state in what is now Turkey which was besieged by the Greeks for ten years to capture the beautiful Helen.

The other outstanding find was a red-figured Attic kylix (drinking cup) showing a sacrificial procession and

the photographic drill before digging began.

Hercules struggling with a sea god named Nereus. This has been attributed to one of the most famous artists of Athens, Oltos, who lived in the early fifth century B.C.

These and many other discoveries are on display at the Villa Giulia.

While the work was going on in the Tarquinia necropolises, the robberies by the tombaroli were reduced to only a few pilfered tombs a year, but when the team of experts moved on to other sites, the tomb robbing began again with the authorities apparently unable to control or prevent it.

Scene from Greek kylix, painted by Oltos.
Found in Tomb 610 at Cerveteri.

During the explorations at Vulci, a five-chambered tomb was discovered. This raised high hopes of furnishing new clues to the enigma of the Etruscan language, for the tomb contained many inscriptions in both Latin and Etruscan. Here at last could be the long-sought bilingual text which might prove to be the needed Rosetta Stone to unlock the secret. But alas, this was not the case. Further study disclosed that the tomb had been used for several generations of families during the transition from Etruscan to Roman rule. The late inscriptions were all in Latin and had no relation to the earlier Etruscan ones.

Prospecting began in the Tarquinia necropolis in 1956 and continued without interruption for eight years. It was here that the famed Tomb of the Olympics was discovered with its lively representations of Etruscan athletes running, throwing the discus, and racing spirited horses.

Altogether, seventy painted tombs have been discovered at Tarquinia by these new scientific methods since the Tomb of the Olympics was unearthed. Undoubtedly many more remain to be found and their paintings protected before they are vandalized by man or inadvertently harmed in the name of what is called progress. The expansion of towns located in Etruscan areas, new highway construction, the establishment of industrial plants and public works, the deep working of the soil in districts of land reclamation—all contribute to the deterioration or destruction of the remains of ancient civilizations buried underground.

Intensive farming, which has spread to the most valuable archaeological zones, in particular Cerveteri and Tarquinia, continues to damage tombs. Nitrogenous fertilizers mixed with rainwater seep into the underground chambers, causing saltpeter deposits on the walls; roots of plants force their way downward into the tombs, causing other damage. Unfortunately, the Italian government has not sufficient funds for the expropriation of these lands to prevent further destruction.

In 1968, during excavations at the hillside necropolis of Tuscania, forty miles north of Rome, an exciting discovery was made: a chamber tomb in which were found tightly packed together ten sarcophagi with recumbent figures on their lids. These were all members of a single family, the Corunas, according to the inscriptions. One, Setre Corunas, was a thickset gentleman in a toga which leaves bare his fat stomach to the navel. He has a double chin and undoubtedly looked exactly like this in life. Beside him was his wife, Apunia Panaquilla, a forceful-looking lady in her forties who seems ready to spring up from the couch as if alerted by a sudden noise. The tomb had been looted of everything removable, but the sarcophagi with their carved lids and lifelike figures were too heavy for the tombaroli. Instead they hacked holes in the corners of the lids into which they could sink their arms in search of jewels.

The account of this find was published in an information pamphlet called "The Italian Scene" distributed by the Istituto di Cultura in Rome. Written in sprightly

Figure from a sarcophagus lid, known as "The Obese Etruscan," who lived during the time of Etruscan domination by Rome. Note the patera in his right hand duplicated by the ring on his finger.

style it tells how "the assistant archaeologist who first beamed his flashlight into the darkness of the tomb . . . got the shock of his life as he picked out what appeared to be a crowd of persons all rising on their elbows as if startled by the sudden intrusion. The head of the family, Setre, looked especially lifelike, proffering a bowl with coins with which he intended to pay his way into the Nether World. The bowl, alas, was empty. Somebody long long ago had deprived Setre of the money for his ticket."

XII

The Story That Has No End

The mystery of the Etruscans is still unsolved. Our present knowledge is like a partially completed mosaic of many bits and pieces of colored stones with blank areas where stones to finish the picture are missing. But the search for the needed pieces goes on.

Archaeologists are constantly investigating new sites, finding new tombs, seeking new clues. Some happy day, distant or soon, they may come upon the ruins of an Etruscan town buried below the brambles and scrub of an empty hilltop or plateau where no later town has grown up upon its rubble to make excavation difficult or impossible. If and when such a find is made, archaeologists hope to discover inscriptions in Latin and in Etruscan side by side, pertaining to some civic event which will provide new words for the sparse Etruscan vocabulary which additional funerary epitaphs fail to do.

With the new tools science has provided, the archaeologists may yet discover, stored safely away in some underground hiding place, the long-lost history of the Etruscan people written centuries ago by the Emperor Claudius. Unlikely as that is, stranger things have happened.

There is a wealth of unprobed territory. The whole lovely land of Italy is layered with older civilizations beneath its surface, some of them in unpopulated areas. Difficulty comes when villages or private farmlands are in the way of the archaeologists' shovels, or there is a lack of funds to finance exploration.

Another source of archaeological wealth lies under the waters that lap the shores of Italy. Sunken wrecks abound in these seas, the remains of thousands of ships that plied the coastwise routes carrying cargoes for trade between the east and west. Historical sources provide clues to the location of some of these, but the older wrecks are most often found by chance when fishnets become entangled in the wreckage.

The wooden frames of many ancient ships have almost completely disintegrated. Often only the metal parts remain and the kinds of freight which were unaffected by the corrosive action of sea water and the erosive damage caused by currents.

Although the entire archaeological wealth of Italy, including discoveries made in territorial waters, is by law the property of the state (with the exception of private collections created before 1939), hundreds of skin divers have explored wrecks in shallow waters and have appropriated their finds either for their own delight or to sell for profit. This lack of respect for the law relating to antiquities is one of the continuing problems that the Ancient Monuments Administration has been unable to solve.

On land, tomb-robbing is an occupation that has been pursued for centuries and followed by successive generations of the same peasant families. It can truly be said that "tombaroli are born, not made." During the season of heavy work in the fields at springtime and harvest, their illegal activities decrease. But only temporarily. When there is no other work, grave-robbing is the occupation they follow. Today many of them are up-to-date in their methods, using power drills and disc or wire saws to remove paintings from walls. In addition to cheating their country of the works of art they steal, they do irreparable damage to the objects and make more difficult the search for knowledge.

Carlo Lerici estimates that the damage and loss each year caused by illicit digging amounts to some three or four billion lira. In American money this would be roughly three to four million dollars. He bases these figures on the international market prices of smuggled works of art at open auction sales. The ironic thing is that the tombaroli receive only a small percentage of this. Those who profit most are the receivers of the stolen objects, the exporters, and the dealers.

The least unhappy aspect of this situation is that many

wonderful objects would remain buried underground indefinitely or would vanish into the storehouses of Italian museums—which are already overcrowded with material and haven't the funds to study, classify, or restore the antiquities—if it weren't for the tombaroli. As it is, reputable museums and collectors in other countries acquire these objects and make them available for many to enjoy. But the economic loss to Italy is great.

Clandestine digging has spawned another evil, the perpetration of forgeries. A modern imitation of an Etruscan vase or a bronze figurine will be buried in the earth and then dug up after it has been suitably "aged" and offered in a newspaper-wrapped package to the unwary tourist as the real thing. The purchaser, if he discovers he has been fooled, is in a dilemma. He cannot go to the authorities to report the fraud, for he would then have to admit that he bought illegally what he thought was a genuine work of Etruscan art.

Even museums have been taken in. The Metropolitan Museum of Art in New York City purchased in good faith three enormous terra cotta statues of helmeted warriors, identified as Etruscan works of the sixth or fifth century B.C. They were put on display and were much admired from 1933 until 1961, when the museum itself found them to be forgeries. It turned out that they were the creation of a man from near Orvieto, Italy, and his two cousins, who had made them during the years of the First World War, then hammered them into splinters or potsherds and buried them. Later, when they dug them up and pieced them together, they proclaimed a great discovery.

Years after the figures had been purchased by the New York museum, a Roman taxi driver, who had aided in their construction, boasted about his share in the work with the pride of a craftsman, and then basked in the attendant publicity. Then the Metropolitan found out that it had been hoaxed. The warriors were left on display for a while after they made the headlines, then were quietly withdrawn. But perhaps they served a purpose in making the public aware of the dangers of forgery in Etruscan art.

Interest in the Etruscans grows. They exert a fascination, produce a desire to know more. As unlike the Romans as the Romans were unlike the Greeks, the Etruscans have survived the oblivion which submerged them for seventeen centuries. Etruscan blood, even though diluted, still flows in the veins of the people of Tuscany and may be identified in the proud profile of an occasional peasant.

The lovely objects they created to accompany their dead—the bronze figures, the ceramic statues, the exquisite and delicate gold jewelry, the vases, mirrors, weapons, bas-reliefs, all wrought with loving skill and care, but most especially the wall paintings—speak eloquently of their once glorious past, of their joy in life, and their triumph over death.